D1647703

5-Minute
Daily
Prayer
Journal

5-Minute
Daily
Prayer
Journal

Reflections and Scripture for a Deeper Faith

JOCASTA ODOM

ROCKRIDGE
PRESS

Copyright © 2021 by Rockridge Press, Emeryville, California

No part of this publication may be reproduced, stored in a retrieval system, or trans-mitted in any form or by any means, electronic, mechanical, photocopying, recording, scanning, or otherwise, except as permitted under Sections 107 or 108 of the 1976 United States Copyright Act, without the prior written permission of the Publisher. Requests to the Publisher for permission should be addressed to the Permissions Department, Rockridge Press, 6005 Shellmound Street, Suite 175, Emeryville, CA 94608.

Limit of Liability/Disclaimer of Warranty: The Publisher and the author make no repre-sentations or warranties with respect to the accuracy or completeness of the contents of this work and specifically disclaim all warranties, including without limitation warran-ties of fitness for a particular purpose. No warranty may be created or extended by sales or promotional materials. The advice and strategies contained herein may not be suitable for every situation. This work is sold with the understanding that the Publisher is not engaged in rendering medical, legal, or other professional advice or services. If professional assistance is required, the services of a competent professional person should be sought. Neither the Publisher nor the author shall be liable for damages arising herefrom. The fact that an individual, organization, or website is referred to in this work as a citation and/or potential source of further information does not mean that the author or the Publisher endorses the information the individual, organization, or website may provide or recommendations they/it may make. Further, readers should be aware that websites listed in this work may have changed or disappeared between when this work was written and when it is read.

For general information on our other products and services or to obtain technical support, please contact our Customer Care Department within the United States at (866) 744-2665, or outside the United States at (510) 253-0500.

Rockridge Press publishes its books in a variety of electronic and print formats. Some content that appears in print may not be available in electronic books, and vice versa.

TRADEMARKS: Rockridge Press and the Rockridge Press logo are trademarks or reg-istered trademarks of Callisto Media Inc. and/or its affiliates, in the United States and other countries, and may not be used without written permission. All other trademarks are the property of their respective owners. Rockridge Press is not associated with any product or vendor mentioned in this book.

Interior and Cover Designer: Lisa Schreiber
Art Producer: Meg Baggott
Editor: Kelly Koester
Production Editor: Ruth Sakata Corley

Cover and interior photos used under license from iStock Photo.
Author photo courtesy of Leonard King / Eye-So Keen Photography

ISBN: Print 978-1-64876-094-5

R0

*This book is dedicated to my
mother, Sheila Smith Gates. She
taught me the importance of being
an educated, supportive, loving, caring,
empowering, and goal-oriented woman
of God. She taught me to find strength in
my weaknesses and spread love to the
masses. She always said when we end
our conversations we will never say
"goodbye," but always "I love you."
Mom, I love you.*

This journal belongs to:

Contents

ADVERSITY

COMMUNICATION

DOUBT

LOVE

Continued on next page

STRENGTH

Continued on next page

Introduction

Welcome to your Daily Prayer Journal, a devotional for you to make time for God's word. With only five minutes a day, this journal will provide you with peace, understanding, and a closer relationship with Him. A prayer journal like this allows you to write down your prayers and make them plain, like mentioned in Habakkuk 2:2: "Write the vision and make it plain on tablets." Consider this your modern-day tablet.

My best friend of 32 years and I stay connected through God's word and the weekly Bible study we have together. We both write down other people's prayer requests. My friend not only writes down the requests but also will check back on them periodically. Once they are answered, he makes a record in his journal. This journal has a section where you, too, can record your answered prayers and make notes on when you feel God has spoken to you.

The journal is broken down into 10 themes—trust, faith, adversity, communication, doubt, love, wisdom, strength, hope, and forgiveness. Every entry will start with a message from scripture. You will be asked to reflect on how the scripture might apply to you in real life. Use the provided space to respond. There will be a topic at the end of each entry either asking you to write down prayer requests, your blessings, things you can give thanks for, or what kinds of things you might ask for guidance about. Those four topics rotate throughout the journal.

Now get ready to take your first step in a journey toward a daily life filled with Christ. God Bless!

Put Your Trust in God

Trust in the Lord with all your heart, And lean not on your own under-standing; In all your ways acknowledge Him, And He shall direct your paths. PROVERBS 3:5–6 (NKJV)

Reflection: "Did I pick the right career?" "Am I a good enough parent?" "What should I do now?" While life can be filled with doubt, the trust you place in the Lord will never lead you astray. Even if your paths feel crooked, God is overseeing every step.

What or who do you usually trust? Is it hard for you to trust that prayers will be answered? Explain some steps you will take to begin to trust God more.

_____

_____

_____

_____

_____

PRAYER REQUESTS _____

_____

_____

_____

_____

_____

Moving Mountains

Jesus replied, "Truly I tell you, if you have faith and do not doubt . . . you can say to this mountain, 'Go throw yourself into the sea,' and it will be done. If you believe, you will receive whatever you ask for in prayer."
MATTHEW 21:21–22 (NIV)

Reflection: Challenges like losing a job or having someone close fall ill can feel like life has placed a mountain in front of you. Remember to trust in the Lord. With Him, you can overcome any obstacle.

What mountain(s) have you faced or are you facing? How can you ask God for (specific) help?

_____

_____

_____

_____

_____

BLESSINGS _____

_____

_____

_____

_____

_____

_____

The Greatest Power

And now abide faith, hope, love, these three; but the greatest of these is love. 1 CORINTHIANS 13:13 (NKJV)

Reflection: Broken hearts, harsh words, misunderstandings . . . they can hurt so deeply. God provided you an example of ultimate love; use this love to get through the pain.

Why is love important in life? How has God revealed His love to you?

_____

_____

_____

_____

_____

_____

THANKS _____

_____

_____

_____

_____

_____

_____

_____

_____

God's Word Is Clear

So then faith comes by hearing, and hearing by the word of God.
ROMANS 10:17 (NKJV)

Reflection: Crowds, meetings, traffic. The hustle and bustle of the world can drown out the voice of God. Taking time to be still and read God's word, even five minutes a day, will allow you to hear His voice.

What do you need to do to unplug? How will you begin to make time to listen—and hear—from God?

_____

_____

_____

_____

_____

GUIDANCE _____

_____

_____

_____

_____

_____

_____

The Wise Applies

If any of you lacks wisdom, let him ask of God, who gives to all liberally and without reproach, and it will be given to him. JAMES 1:5 (NKJV)

Reflection: With God's wisdom upon you, you can go forth and be great in this world. You only have to ask.

How can you gain wisdom? Where do you need insight?

_____

_____

_____

_____

_____

PRAYER REQUESTS _____

_____

_____

_____

_____

_____

_____

_____

_____

Practice God, Seek God

But without faith it is impossible to please Him, for he who comes to God must believe that He is, and that He is a rewarder of those who diligently seek Him. HEBREWS 11:6 (NKJV)

Reflection: If you want to learn a new language, you have to study it but also practice it. Only reading a book won't work. The same is true about seeking God. You must seek Him with all of you.

How do you diligently seek God?

_____

_____

_____

_____

_____

BLESSINGS _____

_____

_____

_____

_____

_____

_____

_____

Ask to Receive

God is our refuge and strength, A very present help in trouble.
PSALM 46:1 (NKJV)

Reflection: People aren't mind readers. To get help, you have to ask for it. It can be the same with prayer. Sure, God already knows what is best for you and is on your side. But tell Him your exact troubles. Ask for specific help. He will be there.

Where do you need help, and who besides God can you ask? How has God helped you in your time of need?

_____

_____

_____

_____

_____

THANKS _____

_____

_____

_____

_____

_____

_____

Looking Away

Therefore let us, as many as are mature, have this mind; and if in anything you think otherwise, God will reveal even this to you.
PHILIPPIANS 3:15 (NKJV)

Reflection: Distractions will come, but don't let them deter you from your blessed future. Stay focused on God's promises. Stay focused on your goals.

What goals has God set for your life? Take a minute to intentionally set your day with them in mind.

_____

_____

_____

_____

_____

GUIDANCE _____

_____

_____

_____

_____

_____

_____

_____

_____

Find Your Happy Space

Happy are the people who are in such a state; Happy are the people whose God is the Lord! PSALM 144:15 (NKJV)

Reflection: Look for happiness in the simple things God provides for you in things money can't buy.

Where is your happy space? What do you do there?

_____

_____

_____

_____

_____

_____

PRAYER REQUESTS ⎯⎯⎯⎯⎯⎯⎯⎯⎯⎯⎯⎯⎯

_____

_____

_____

_____

_____

_____

_____

_____

_____

_____

It Is Your Season

To everything there is a season, A time for every purpose under heaven: A time to be born, And a time to die; A time to plant, And a time to pluck what is planted; A time to kill, And a time to heal; A time to break down, And a time to build up. ECCLESIASTES 3:1–3 (NKJV)

Reflection: This is your time to shine and let go of anything stopping you from being "great." God has set this season out just for you.

Make a list of things you want to fulfill in this "right time" season.

_____

_____

_____

_____

_____

BLESSINGS _____

_____

_____

_____

_____

_____

_____

_____

_____

Made in God's Image

So God created man in His own image; in the image of God He created him; male and female He created them. GENESIS 1:27 (NKJV)

Reflection: The world has made you feel like image is everything. Yet, we all were made in the image of God. Therefore, we are not defined by this world; God defines us. You are His perfect creation.

Do you sometimes allow the world to define you? Why?

_____

_____

_____

_____

_____

THANKS _____

_____

_____

_____

_____

_____

_____

_____

_____

God Gives You Peace

Peace I leave with you, My peace I give to you; not as the world gives do I give to you. Let not your heart be troubled, neither let it be afraid.
JOHN 14:27 (NKJV)

Reflection: God has told you He will give you peace amid trouble. He will cover you in your weakest moments and calm you from worldly distractions.

Make a list of areas in your life where you want God to provide peace. Be specific, such as "God, provide peace in my marriage."

_____

_____

_____

_____

_____

GUIDANCE

12

Beauty Goes Deeper Than Looks

Charm is deceitful and beauty is passing, But a woman who fears the Lord, she shall be praised. PROVERBS 31:30 (NKJV)

Reflection: Growing old is inevitable. Although beauty will fade, the comfort in knowing Jesus will be everlasting. The way people see Jesus through you is a beauty deeper than looks.

What can you do to place more focus on singing God's praises?

_____

_____

_____

_____

_____

PRAYER REQUESTS _____

_____

_____

_____

_____

_____

_____

_____

_____

Leave Behind the Old

Therefore, if anyone is in Christ, he is a new creation; old things have passed away; behold, all things have become new.
2 CORINTHIANS 5:17 (NKJV)

Reflection: Although we are often reminded of our past mistakes, they do not define our present. When you accepted Jesus, you left the old you behind and became a new person. Try to see only your present looking toward your future.

How will you begin to walk into the newness of how God created you?

_____

_____

_____

_____

_____

BLESSINGS _____

_____

_____

_____

_____

_____

_____

Unseen and Real

Now faith is the substance of things hoped for, the evidence of things not seen. HEBREWS 11:1 (NKJV)

Reflection: While you cannot see oxygen, you know it exists and understand the importance of it to live. Faith is your oxygen and connection to Jesus.

Does your faith provide you with Hope? Has your faith ever been tested? If so, when, and how did you handle it?

_____

_____

_____

_____

_____

_____

THANKS _____

_____

_____

_____

_____

_____

_____

_____

Roar! Your Strength Is from Jesus

I can do all things through Christ who strengthens me.
PHILIPPIANS 4:13 (NKJV)

Reflection: We cannot forget our strength comes from Jesus. When overwhelmed or feeling down, call on the Lord. He will renew your strength at all times. Our Lord and Savior will never let us fall.

What can you do to deepen your commitment to your faith?

_____

_____

_____

_____

_____

GUIDANCE _____

_____

_____

_____

_____

_____

_____

Keep the Faith

Have faith in God," Jesus answered . . . I tell you, whatever you ask for in prayer, believe that you have received it, and it will be yours.
MARK 11:22–24 (NIV)

Reflection: God will provide the desires of the heart as long as you just "keep the faith." Believe that you will receive it.

What does your heart desire? Be specific.

_____

_____

_____

_____

_____

_____

PRAYER REQUESTS _____

_____

_____

_____

_____

_____

_____

_____

_____

Kindness Goes a Long Way

And be kind to one another, tenderhearted, forgiving one another, even as God in Christ forgave you. EPHESIANS 4:32 (NKJV)

Reflection: When we repent, God forgives us. Yet, sometimes when others ask for our forgiveness, we aren't as forgiving. Wouldn't God want us to be kind to everyone no matter the circumstances?

How will you pattern your life toward being as forgiving as God? Who can you forgive *today*?

_____

_____

_____

_____

_____

BLESSINGS _____

_____

_____

_____

_____

_____

_____

Knowledge Brings Understanding

Happy is the man who finds wisdom, And the man who gains understanding . . . PROVERBS 3:13 (NKJV)

Reflection: Through wisdom you receive understanding; they go together. We must not only want to *receive* understanding but also *provide* understanding. Our challenge is to listen to understand, and not listen to respond.

When was the last disagreement you had? Were you actively listening or waiting for your chance to speak? How can you change that habit?

_____

_____

_____

_____

_____

THANKS _____

_____

_____

_____

_____

_____

Encouragement Is Refreshing

Therefore encourage one another and build each other up, just as in fact you are doing. 1 THESSALONIANS 5:11 (NIV)

Reflection: Doesn't it feel good when other people encourage you and give you a boost of assurance? Be sure to encourage others, too, during good and bad times. Encouragement is refreshing, especially when it is shared daily.

Who do you encourage? Think of a friend or family member who may need some encouragement. List ways you can reach out to them today.

_____

_____

_____

_____

_____

GUIDANCE _____

_____

_____

_____

_____

_____

_____

_____

Rejoice Daily

This is the day the Lord has made; We will rejoice and be glad in it.
PSALM 118:24 (NKJV)

Reflection: Today doesn't just have to mean work. We can rejoice, because the sun and sky provide us with beauty for the day. The trees provide us with a breeze. The clouds provide us peaceful beauty. When it rains, God provides us the hope of growth.

How can you rejoice today in the beauty of the earth, and focus less on the distractions of the calendar?

_____

_____

_____

_____

_____

PRAYER REQUESTS _____

_____

_____

_____

_____

_____

_____

God Will Protect You

The Lord is my light and my salvation; Whom shall I fear? The Lord is the strength of my life; Of whom shall I be afraid? PSALM 27:1 (NKJV)

Reflection: The Lord will keep you safe in His arms. Stand firm on His words. God is your light in the midst of darkness, leading you to safety.

When was a time you needed God, and He kept you safe? If you need safety now, how can God help?

_____

_____

_____

_____

_____

BLESSINGS _____

_____

_____

_____

_____

_____

_____

_____

Test the Spirit by the Spirit

Beloved, do not believe every spirit, but test the spirits, whether they are of God; because many false prophets have gone out into the world.
1 JOHN 4:1 (NKJV)

Reflection: Surrounding yourself with people who share your faith will uplift you and enrich your life. If you're having trouble finding others with like values, join groups at church like a Bible study.

What steps will you take to be around more likeminded, Christian people?

_____

_____

_____

_____

_____

THANKS _____

_____

_____

_____

_____

_____

_____

_____

_____

Jesus Will Show You the Way

Being confident of this very thing, that He who has begun a
good work in you will complete it until the day of Jesus Christ.
PHILIPPIANS 1:6 (NKJV)

Reflection: God has a plan for you. If He has called you to lead at work or at church, be confident that you can do it. He believes in you so you should too!

When did someone else believe in you before you believed in yourself? How did it help?

_____

_____

_____

_____

_____

GUIDANCE ———————————————————————

_____

_____

_____

_____

_____

_____

The Tiniest Faith Takes You Far

So Jesus said to them, "Because of your unbelief; for assuredly,
I say to you, if you have faith as a mustard seed, you will say to this
mountain, 'Move from here to there,' and it will move; and nothing
will be impossible for you." MATTHEW 17:20 (NKJV)

Reflection: We often think we have to make big changes to get big results. But sometimes *any* change can make a difference. Rounding up some mustard seed–sized faith can turn a glass that's half empty into one that's half full.

What can you do to build up your faith?

_____

_____

_____

_____

_____

PRAYER REQUESTS _____

_____

_____

_____

_____

_____

Hope Is Fulfilling

Blessed is the man who trusts in the Lord, And whose hope is the Lord.
JEREMIAH 17:7 (NKJV)

Reflection: Placing hope in the Lord means trusting He will never fail you. People in the world ask for much more and provide much less. Why not place your hope in the Lord?

What is holding your hope hostage?

_____

_____

_____

_____

_____

BLESSINGS ———————————————————

_____

_____

_____

_____

_____

_____

_____

_____

_____

Believe It

And whatever things you ask in prayer, believing, you will receive.
MATTHEW 21:22 (NKJV)

Reflection: God is eager to hear from you! He is patiently waiting for you to speak to Him about your needs. Prayer is a powerful tool that can be used anywhere, anytime. You can pray while making breakfast, cleaning, brushing your teeth, even during television commercials.

What role does prayer serve in your belief system? Has God answered you in prayer recently?

_____

_____

_____

_____

_____

THANKS _____

_____

_____

_____

_____

_____

_____

Inner Strength

I keep my eyes always on the Lord. With him at my right hand, I will not be shaken. PSALM 16:8 (NIV)

Reflection: God will fight when you feel as though you have lost the battle. God did not create you in His image to lose. Pick up your head and allow Him to show you your path. You are a Warrior!

Do you sometimes forget your strength is from the Lord? What can you do to build your strength?

_____

_____

_____

_____

_____

GUIDANCE _____

_____

_____

_____

_____

_____

_____

You Won't Be Stranded

And the Lord, He is the One who goes before you. He will be with you, He will not leave you nor forsake you; do not fear nor be dismayed.
DEUTERONOMY 31:8 (NKJV)

Reflection: God has met your troubles head-on, and He will conquer them all with you. God will not leave you stranded; His love for you is too great.

Who do you consider to be your support system? Recall a time when God went before you, as in scripture.

_____

_____

_____

_____

_____

_____

PRAYER REQUESTS ———————————————————————

_____

_____

_____

_____

_____

_____

_____

_____

Increased Faith Decreases Doubt

And immediately Jesus stretched out His hand and caught him, and said to him, "O you of little faith, why did you doubt?" MATTHEW 14:31 (NKJV)

Reflection: Doubt will seep into a place with a cracked foundation. If your foundation is built strong by Jesus Christ, faith will slay all doubt.

When was the last time you doubted yourself? Why?

_____

_____

_____

_____

_____

BLESSINGS _____

_____

_____

_____

_____

_____

_____

_____

Grace Is Sufficient

For by grace you have been saved through faith, and that not of your-selves; it is the gift of God, not of works, lest anyone should boast.
EPHESIANS 2:8–9 (NKJV)

Reflection: Grace is a gift that God gave to the world. It belongs to everyone.

How do you think of grace? Why did God extend us His grace? How has He given you grace?

_____

_____

_____

_____

_____

THANKS _____

_____

_____

_____

_____

_____

_____

You Are Jesus's Treasure

Look at the birds of the air, for they neither sow nor reap nor gather into barns; yet your heavenly Father feeds them. Are you not of more value than they? MATTHEW 6:26 (NKJV)

Reflection: Jesus treasures you deeply. Your mere presence adds to the kingdom. Even if you feel disliked, Jesus loves you. You are valuable.

How do you add your value to the kingdom?

_____

_____

_____

_____

_____

GUIDANCE

_____

_____

_____

_____

_____

_____

_____

_____

Live Out His Plans for You

"For I know the plans I have for you," declares the Lord, "plans to prosper you and not to harm you, plans to give you hope and a future."
JEREMIAH 29:11 (NIV)

Reflection: God set plans for you even before you were born. He wants you to prosper in all aspects of life: careers, family, friendships, and more. Will there be downturns and pitfalls? Yes. But God wants you to know He provides for your future.

How will you allow God to plan your future? How have you seen some plans already come to light?

_____

_____

_____

_____

_____

_____

PRAYER REQUESTS ━━━━━━━━━━━━━━━━━━━━━━━

_____

_____

_____

_____

_____

_____

Finish the Race

I have fought the good fight, I have finished the race, I have kept the faith.
2 TIMOTHY 4:7 (NIV)

Reflection: When you're running a race, you keep going until the finish line. But often we are given a task and when it gets hard, we give up. When God is running with you, He will give you the strength to finish the race.

How can you use your faith to get you past the feeling of giving up?

_____

_____

_____

_____

_____

BLESSINGS _____

_____

_____

_____

_____

_____

_____

Sing God's Praises

Let my mouth be filled with Your praise And with Your glory all the day.
PSALM 71:8 (NKJV)

Reflection: When you wake up, begin with praises to the Lord. The day is busy, but it can be less overwhelming if we start it with praise. Praise Him for waking you up. Praise Him for the day. You'll be amazed at how much better your day will go.

How can you incorporate a daily praise into your life?

_____

_____

_____

_____

_____

THANKS _____

_____

_____

_____

_____

_____

_____

_____

Still Standing

Be on your guard; stand firm in the faith; be courageous; be strong.
1 CORINTHIANS 16:13 (NIV)

Reflection: People are sometimes overlooked for their resilience and hard work. We are stronger than we realize.

When was a recent time you showed courage and strength? How do you stand firm in your faith?

_____

_____

_____

_____

_____

GUIDANCE _____

_____

_____

_____

_____

_____

_____

_____

_____

_____

Allow Yourself to Live

For sin shall not have dominion over you, for you are not under law but under grace. ROMANS 6:14 (NKJV)

Reflection: Even if things remind us of our sins, if we have repented, we can move forward and live under grace. Our sin is not our end! Six words: *Thank you, God, for your grace.*

Do you try to repent daily? If not, how can you start?

_____

_____

_____

_____

_____

_____

_____

_____

_____

_____

_____

_____

_____

_____

_____

Healing through Faith

Then Jesus said to him, "Go your way; your faith has made you well."
And immediately he received his sight and followed Jesus on the road.
MARK 10:52 (NKJV)

Reflection: Faith has unspeakable power. Sometimes we are spiritually blind and cannot see due to life's cloudy view. Jesus can remove the clouds and give you sight.

Has Jesus helped heal you? When has Jesus cleared your view and given you sight?

_____

_____

_____

_____

_____

BLESSINGS _____

_____

_____

_____

_____

_____

_____

Faith and Action

In the same way, faith by itself, if it is not accompanied by action, is dead.
JAMES 2:17 (NIV)

Reflection: Would you expect no cavities if you never brush your teeth? Probably not. Same with applying faith—it takes action on our part. When you ask God for something, you also have to take action. Putting in the work is part of being a faithful servant.

What have you asked God for recently? Along with your faith, what other work did you do to help make it happen?

_____

_____

_____

_____

_____

THANKS _____

_____

_____

_____

_____

_____

_____

_____

Unconditional Love

For God so loved the world, that he gave his only begotten Son, that whosoever believeth in him should not perish, but have everlasting life.
JOHN 3:16 (NKJV)

Reflection: God's unconditional love reigns forever. Really think about this: He brought His only son into our world, knowing He would be treated the way He was, in order for us to have everlasting life. God loves us so much.

Do you feel the power of love? What does God's love mean to you?

_____

_____

_____

_____

_____

GUIDANCE _____

_____

_____

_____

_____

_____

_____

_____

Ask and You Will Receive

Therefore I tell you, whatever you ask for in prayer, believe that you have received it, and it will be yours. MARK 11:24 (NIV)

Reflection: To ask and receive is a great way to have your needs met. This can apply to speaking to God, but also with people in your life. Speak up for yourself and say what your needs are.

Is there someone you can better communicate your needs to? What about to God?

_____

_____

_____

_____

_____

PRAYER REQUESTS _____

_____

_____

_____

_____

_____

_____

_____

_____

This Too Shall Pass

Commit your way to the Lord, Trust also in Him, And He shall bring it to pass. PSALM 37:5 (NKJV)

Reflection: Commitment can be hard for some and easy for others. Even if you are struggling with sticking to a commitment, remember that Jesus is with you through thick and thin. He is even with you as you work toward honoring your commitments.

Are there commitments you are struggling to honor? How can Jesus help?

_____

_____

_____

_____

_____

BLESSINGS _____

_____

_____

_____

_____

_____

_____

_____

Speaking Softly

A soft answer turns away wrath, but a harsh word stirs up anger.
PROVERBS 15:1 (ESV)

Reflection: Screamers may be loud, and they may be heard, but rarely are they listened to. A softer, more nurturing voice can often be more powerful and command a room. It can provide peace in the midst of chaos.

Do you sometimes speak harshly toward others? What are some ways you can remember to speak softly and calmly?

_____

_____

_____

_____

_____

THANKS _____

_____

_____

_____

_____

_____

_____

_____

Sins Are Heavy Weights

Then he adds: "Their sins and lawless acts I will remember no more."
HEBREWS 10:17 (NIV)

Reflection: The hardest thing to do is to forgive ourselves for our sins. If Jesus can forgive us, though, why do we think we can't? Surely His opinion has more weight. You have the control to repent and let go of the burden.

Do you hold your self-forgiveness hostage? How can you begin to forgive yourself as God forgives you?

_____

_____

_____

_____

_____

GUIDANCE _____

_____

_____

_____

_____

_____

_____

_____

Lead with Love

Let all that you do be done with love. 1 CORINTHIANS 16:14 (NKJV)

Reflection: Repeat this to yourself every so often: Dear God, I know Your love has the power to rule the world. Help me use that love to push out any hate or trouble I may carry in my heart. Help me lead my life with love. Amen.

What are some ways you can lead your life with love?

_____

_____

_____

_____

_____

PRAYER REQUESTS ————————————————————

_____

_____

_____

_____

_____

_____

_____

_____

Jesus Is Shelter

It is better to take refuge in the Lord than to trust in man. PSALM 118:8 (NKJV)

Reflection: We've all been disappointed. Promises broken, things lost, deadlines missed. Three who haven't let us down? The Holy Trinity of Father, Son, and Holy Spirit.

What are you needing refuge from? What kind of shelter are you looking for?

_____

_____

_____

_____

_____

BLESSINGS _____

_____

_____

_____

_____

_____

_____

_____

_____

Prayer Is a Lifestyle

Rejoice always, pray continually, give thanks in all circumstances; for this is God's will for you in Christ Jesus. 1 THESSALONIANS 5:16–18 (NIV)

Reflection: Prayer is a great way to communicate directly with God. It can be in the form of, "traffic is light today, thank you Jesus." Or, "I am about to lose my temper. Help me!" Think of it as a never-ending inner dialogue with your very best friend.

Do you have a prayer schedule in your life? If not, try and start one! Make a prayer list below.

THANKS

God Will Instruct You

The fear of the Lord is the beginning of knowledge; fools despise wisdom and instruction. PROVERBS 1:7 (ESV)

Reflection: We already have the instructions we need to live a faithful and fulfilling life. The simple awareness of God in our life is the first step in finding those instructions to follow.

How has your awareness of God in your life grown since you started this journal?

_____

_____

_____

_____

_____

GUIDANCE _____

_____

_____

_____

_____

_____

_____

_____

_____

Rise above Adversity

We are hard pressed on every side, but not crushed; perplexed, but not in despair; persecuted, but not abandoned; struck down, but not destroyed. We always carry around in our body the death of Jesus, so that the life of Jesus may also be revealed in our body. 2 CORINTHIANS 4:8–10 (NIV)

Reflection: Through every troubling situation, you persevere by carrying the Lord within you. He died for us to live for us.

How do you reveal the life of Jesus to others? Can they see the life of Jesus within you?

_____

_____

_____

_____

_____

PRAYER REQUESTS ⎯⎯⎯⎯⎯⎯⎯⎯⎯⎯⎯⎯⎯⎯⎯⎯⎯⎯⎯⎯⎯⎯

_____

_____

_____

_____

_____

_____

_____

_____

Suffering Does Not Last

And the God of all grace, who called you to his eternal glory in Christ, after you have suffered a little while, will himself restore you and make you strong, firm and steadfast. 1 PETER 5:10 (NIV)

Reflection: Sometimes after a storm, a rainbow appears. It can be a reminder not only of God's beauty but also of His promise to never leave you. Through suffering He will bring you peace. Even through pain, the beauty of God will never cease.

Are you suffering at this moment? How do you think this particular suffering will make you strong, firm, and steadfast?

_____

_____

_____

_____

_____

BLESSINGS ———————————————————————————

_____

_____

_____

_____

_____

_____

Resist Uncertainty

Jesus replied, "You do not realize now what I am doing, but later you will understand." JOHN 13:7 (NIV)

Reflection: We can become uncertain about making so many different decisions in life—from simple ones like deciding what to cook for dinner to more life-altering ones like deciding on children and work. In times of doubt take a deep breath and know God will never place you in a situation you can't handle.

What decisions or situations have you felt uncertain about? What did you decide?

_____

_____

_____

_____

_____

THANKS _____

_____

_____

_____

_____

_____

_____

Finding Comfort in Release

If we confess our sins, He is faithful and just to forgive us our sins and to cleanse us from all unrighteousness. 1 JOHN 1:9 (NKJV)

Reflection: It is comforting to confess and release our sins. It is even more comforting to allow God to guide us away from repeating the same mistakes.

Have you made a mistake recently? What are you doing to prevent repeating that mistake?

GUIDANCE

Start Your Day with God's Love

Let the morning bring me word of your unfailing love, for I have put my trust in you. Show me the way I should go, for to you I entrust my life.
PSALM 143:8 (NIV)

Reflection: Starting your day with God can help show you the way through your day. Wake up with Him and trust His guidance.

Spend a few minutes this morning with God. What kind of guidance can you ask for today?

_____

_____

_____

_____

_____

PRAYER REQUESTS ——————————————————————

_____

_____

_____

_____

_____

_____

_____

_____

_____

More Like Jesus

Jesus said, "Father, forgive them, for they do not know what they are doing." And they divided up his clothes by casting lots. LUKE 23:34 (NIV)

Reflection: Revenge can be tempting. Yet, when Jesus was on the cross He was not thinking about revenge; Jesus was thinking of forgiveness. Remaining focused on the humility Jesus had upon the cross is no easy task.

Have you ever forgiven in your darkest moments? How?

_____

_____

_____

_____

_____

BLESSINGS _____

_____

_____

_____

_____

_____

_____

_____

He Loves You

We love because He first loved us. 1 JOHN 4:19 (NIV)

Reflection: God loves you so much. He has created you in His image to spread His love to the world. Share it with others! God is the originator of "sharing is caring."

How can you help share God's word and spread His love? Be specific.

_____

_____

_____

_____

_____

_____

THANKS _____

_____

_____

_____

_____

_____

_____

_____

_____

_____

Turn Bad News into God News

He is not afraid of bad news; his heart is firm, trusting in the Lord.
PSALM 112:7 (ESV)

Reflection: Although the world presents us with bad news, through prayer and meditation we can find good in the bad. Take bad news and offer it up to God. He will bring solace and peace.

What are you looking forward to God changing in your life?

_____

_____

_____

_____

_____

GUIDANCE _____

_____

_____

_____

_____

_____

_____

_____

_____

Forgiveness Is Immeasurable

Then Peter came up and said to him, "Lord, how often will my brother sin against me, and I forgive him? As many as seven times?" Jesus said to him, "I do not say to you seven times, but seventy times seven."
MATTHEW 18:21–22 (RSV)

Reflection: God never stops forgiving us; shouldn't we do the same?

How many times do you think God has forgiven you? How many times have you forgiven others?

_____

_____

_____

_____

_____

_____

PRAYER REQUESTS

_____

_____

_____

_____

_____

_____

_____

Uplift Others

Let no corrupting talk come out of your mouths, but only such as is good for building up, as fits the occasion, that it may give grace to those who hear. EPHESIANS 4:29 (ESV)

Reflection: Words hold power. Instead of saying, "I can't believe you're running a marathon; that sounds so hard," say, "Wow! I'm so impressed you're running a marathon; what a challenge to take on!" Speaking with love and light can make all the difference.

What words of encouragement can you give someone today?

_____

_____

_____

_____

_____

BLESSINGS

_____

_____

_____

_____

_____

_____

_____

_____

Open-Minded Always

Bearing with one another and, if one has a complaint against another, forgiving each other; as the Lord has forgiven you, so you also must forgive.
COLOSSIANS 3:13 (ESV)

Reflection: Dear God, you call us to remain open-minded about all situations. When someone offends me, help me go directly to them to resolve it peacefully. Help me to resolve complaints and forgive others. Amen.

Will you go to someone to repair the hurt they have caused?

_____

_____

_____

_____

_____

_____

_____

_____

_____

_____

_____

_____

_____

_____

_____

Love for All

To speak evil of no one, to avoid quarreling, to be gentle, and to show perfect courtesy toward all people. TITUS 3:2 (ESV)

Reflection: Any sin committed against you can be forgiven directly through the prayerful love of God and each other. Common courtesy and loving respect for others can create a space for everyone.

When did you feel the power of love recently? How will you show love toward someone today?

_____

_____

_____

_____

_____

GUIDANCE _____

_____

_____

_____

_____

_____

_____

_____

You're Covered

Above all, love each other deeply, because love covers over a multitude of sins. 1 PETER 4:8 (NIV)

Reflection: Love is mentioned over 310 times in the Bible because of its power. Love heals, it renews and restores, and it encourages. Lead with love and you will always win.

Do you love deep? How do you show love to the people most important in your life?

_____

_____

_____

_____

_____

PRAYER REQUESTS _____

_____

_____

_____

_____

_____

_____

_____

_____

Be Selfless

Therefore, confess your sins to one another and pray for one another, that you may be healed. The prayer of a righteous person has great power as it is working. JAMES 5:16 (ESV)

Reflection: Being selfless is a great characteristic. When you are able to pray for someone else you are being selfless. The prayer you provide for another person greatly increases its power.

Do you pray for others? Do you have a prayer list? Make a short one below.

_____

_____

_____

_____

_____

BLESSINGS _____

_____

_____

_____

_____

_____

_____

_____

_____

Safety 101

The fear of man lays a snare, but whoever trusts in the Lord is kept safe.
PROVERBS 29:25 (NIV)

Reflection: Fear can cloud our judgment and make us feel trapped and scared, but trusting in God brings us to safety.

Does God make you feel safe? What has God placed in your life to ease your fears?

_____

_____

_____

_____

_____

THANKS ━━━━━━━━━━━━━━━━━━━━━━━━━━━━━━━

_____

_____

_____

_____

_____

_____

_____

_____

Call His Name

Then you will call upon me and come and pray to me, and I will hear you.
JEREMIAH 29:12 (ESV)

Reflection: God wants to help you! Even silent prayers, held deep in our hearts but never spoken out loud, are heard when we call out His name.

How will you call on God the next time you need help?

_____

_____

_____

_____

_____

GUIDANCE

_____

_____

_____

_____

_____

_____

_____

_____

_____

God Provides Us with Everything

He gives strength to the weary and increases the power of the weak.
ISAIAH 40:29 (NIV)

Reflection: When we hear of God giving us strength, we often picture grand moments or big miracles. But sometimes strength is just getting out of bed in the morning. Or simply saying, "Yes." God's help in our weakest moments might not be glaringly obvious. But it's there.

What kind of strength do you feel in yourself today? Do you need it for something small or something big?

PRAYER REQUESTS

Even Forgiving Foes

But I say to you who hear, Love your enemies, do good to those who hate you . . . LUKE 6:27 (ESV)

Reflection: Forgiving friends and family can be much easier than forgiving a foe. It might take more time and more prayer before it's possible, but trust that it is always possible.

Are you able to offer forgiveness to your enemies?

_____

_____

_____

_____

_____

BLESSINGS _____

_____

_____

_____

_____

_____

_____

_____

_____

Seek Knowledge

An intelligent heart acquires knowledge, and the ear of the wise seeks knowledge. PROVERBS 18:15 (ESV)

Reflection: Does the number of degrees we have determine how smart we are? Maybe, but we can never stop learning. If we read the Bible and regularly go to church, do we know enough about God?

What can you do to gain more biblical knowledge? More ways of the Lord?

_____

_____

_____

_____

_____

_____

THANKS _____

_____

_____

_____

_____

_____

_____

_____

_____

Forgiveness Has No Restraints

He does not deal with us according to our sins, nor repay us according to our iniquities. For as high as the heavens are above the earth, so great is his steadfast love toward those who fear him . . . PSALM 103:10–11 (ESV)

Reflection: God has afforded us the everlasting opportunity to always be forgiven because of His son. Forgiveness has no restraints.

How can you share your story of forgiveness with others?

_____

_____

_____

_____

_____

_____

GUIDANCE _____

_____

_____

_____

_____

_____

_____

_____

_____

_____

Feed My Soul

Gracious words are like a honeycomb, sweetness to the soul and health to the body. PROVERBS 16:24 (ESV)

Reflection: The word of God will feed your Soul. Savor its sweetness.

How does studying the Bible make you feel? What are some of your favorite quotes/passages?

_____

_____

_____

_____

_____

_____

PRAYER REQUESTS

_____

_____

_____

_____

_____

_____

_____

_____

Words and Wisdom

For I will give you words and wisdom that none of your adversaries will be able to resist or contradict. LUKE 21:15 (NIV)

Reflection: Not everyone is a believer. It can be hard to describe or defend why you are a Christian. God's word can be your strongest power. You have a Bible, furnished with words to strengthen you, uplift you, feed you, console you, and support you.

Have you ever quoted scripture to others? What was their response?

_____

_____

_____

_____

_____

BLESSINGS _____

_____

_____

_____

_____

_____

_____

_____

_____

God Is a Soul Speaker

I will praise You, for I am fearfully and wonderfully made; Marvelous are Your works, And that my soul knows very well. PSALM 139:14 (NKJV)

Reflection: You are marvelous. Why? God created you in His image! You are amazing. Why? God molded each part of you so you can be His example of greatness.

How does God speak to your soul? Write something about yourself that you think is marvelous.

THANKS ──────────────────────────────

Your Path Is Clear

For we are His workmanship, created in Christ Jesus for good works, which God prepared beforehand that we should walk in them.
EPHESIANS 2:10 (NKJV)

Reflection: Before you were even born, God cleared a path for you to walk toward your destiny in Heaven. When you doubt it, Jesus's place on the cross should make any doubt disappear.

How do you think God has cleared your path? Where does that path lead?

_____

_____

_____

_____

_____

GUIDANCE _____

_____

_____

_____

_____

_____

_____

_____

Being Understanding

And forgive us our debts, as we also have forgiven our debtors.
MATTHEW 6:12 (ESV)

Reflection: When a friend breaks your trust, you afford them the ability to explain. When you hurt yourself, you need to allow God to forgive and heal you.

Are you understanding toward other people? Has God provided you with the wisdom to understand the benefits of forgiveness?

Faithful to Everyone

Likewise, their wives must be reverent, not slanderers, temperate, faithful in all things. 1 TIMOTHY 3:11 (NKJV)

Reflection: Life brings us so many twists and turns. If we are faithful to Christ and His Commandments, we are able to be faithful to our spouse, children, friends, family, and even our jobs.

What does being "faithful in all things" mean to you? How does this look in your life?

_____

_____

_____

_____

_____

BLESSINGS _____

_____

_____

_____

_____

_____

_____

_____

Cherish the Love of a Friend

A friend loves at all times, And a brother is born for adversity.
PROVERBS 17:17 (NKJV)

Reflection: Friendships allow you to love someone outside of loving yourself, your family, and God. Like God, their love can help you in difficult times.

Which friend helps you in times of adversity? How do you show love in return?

_____

_____

_____

_____

_____

THANKS _____

_____

_____

_____

_____

_____

_____

Being Wise

So shall the knowledge of wisdom be to your soul; If you have found it, there is a prospect, And your hope will not be cut off.
PROVERBS 24:14 (NKJV)

Reflection: People equate wisdom with old age and assume most young people are naive. While experience is certainly a fine teacher, wisdom comes in many forms at any age. Being open to learning is the key.

Do you consider yourself wise? Where do you think you got your wisdom?

_____

_____

_____

_____

_____

GUIDANCE _____

_____

_____

_____

_____

_____

_____

_____

Find Your Strength

For thus says the Lord God, the Holy One of Israel: "In returning and rest you shall be saved; In quietness and confidence shall be your strength."
ISAIAH 30:15 (NKJV)

Reflection: Some think strength comes from being loud, but this is far from the truth. The person who brags the most is often the least confident. When faced with everything in life, being quiet and turning inward to God can be very strengthening.

Do you find strength and confidence in quietness? How can you use this as you face life's challenges?

_____

_____

_____

_____

_____

PRAYER REQUESTS ⎯⎯⎯⎯⎯⎯⎯⎯⎯⎯⎯⎯⎯⎯⎯

_____

_____

_____

_____

_____

_____

_____

Repent Daily

And Peter said to them, "Repent and be baptized every one of you in the name of Jesus Christ for the forgiveness of your sins, and you will receive the gift of the Holy Spirit." ACTS 2:38 (ESV)

Reflection: Asking God for the forgiveness of our sins frees our minds and our hearts. It also allows more room for the Holy Spirit to dwell and grow in us.

How will you make repentance a daily practice?

_____

_____

_____

_____

_____

BLESSINGS _____

_____

_____

_____

_____

_____

_____

Scripture

All Scripture is God-breathed and is useful for teaching, rebuking, correcting and training in righteousness, so that the servant of God may be thoroughly equipped for every good work. 2 TIMOTHY 3:16–17 (NIV)

Reflection: Scripture can be used in many situations, from showing love to your neighbor to asking God to heal your broken heart.

How have you used scripture to teach yourself or to teach others?

THANKS

Never Changing

Jesus Christ is the same yesterday, today, and forever. HEBREWS 13:8 (NKJV)

Reflection: Things can change in an instant. Yet God never changes. God's word is the same today as it was yesterday. He will always remain consistent and intentional.

Are you able to adjust to change? Have you felt God's presence even when there was change around you?

_____

_____

_____

_____

_____

GUIDANCE _____

_____

_____

_____

_____

_____

_____

_____

_____

A Knot for Jesus

Who shall separate us from the love of Christ? Shall tribulation, or distress, or persecution, or famine, or nakedness, or peril, or sword?
ROMANS 8:35 (NKJV)

Reflection: There is a saying that goes "when you are at the end of your rope, tie a knot and hold on." Christ is that knot, refusing to let us go.

Was there a time in your life when something separated you from Jesus? What did you do to get back to Him?

_____

_____

_____

_____

_____

PRAYER REQUESTS ⸻⸻⸻⸻⸻⸻

_____

_____

_____

_____

_____

_____

_____

_____

Paying with Love

In him we have redemption through his blood, the forgiveness of our trespasses, according to the riches of his grace . . . EPHESIANS 1:7 (ESV)

Reflection: While the price Jesus paid for our sins is something we can never repay, we can show Him our love and dedication by living a righteous life. Through His grace we are saved and forgiven—we have been set free.

How do you show your love and dedication to Jesus?

_____

_____

_____

_____

_____

BLESSINGS _____

_____

_____

_____

_____

_____

_____

_____

_____

Friendships Are Precious

Perfume and incense bring joy to the heart, and the pleasantness of a friend springs from their heartfelt advice. PROVERBS 27:9 (NIV)

Reflection: Jesus does not want us to walk through life alone, with no one else to talk to. Look to your friends for more support, more joy, more love.

What friends have been with you through thick and thin?

_____

_____

_____

_____

_____

_____

THANKS _____

_____

_____

_____

_____

_____

_____

_____

_____

God Will Restore You

The Lord is my shepherd; I shall not want. He makes me to lie down in green pastures; He leads me beside the still waters. He restores my soul; He leads me in the paths of righteousness For His name's sake.
PSALM 23:1–3 (NKJV)

Reflection: God will not only protect and provide for you; He will also give you more than you asked for. Not just pastures. Green ones. Waters? Still ones. Your soul? Restored.

What part of your life has God restored?

_____

_____

_____

_____

_____

GUIDANCE _____

_____

_____

_____

_____

_____

_____

Listen to Understand

Listen to advice and accept discipline, and at the end you will be counted among the wise. PROVERBS 19:20 (NIV)

Reflection: Sometimes we ask for advice, then don't follow it. We hear but don't listen. When we really take the time to listen and understand, we are much wiser. Can we be counted among the wise when ignoring sound advice and discipline?

Have you sought advice recently but then not taken it? Why do you think that was?

_____

_____

_____

_____

_____

PRAYER REQUESTS _____

_____

_____

_____

_____

_____

_____

_____

Perfectly Imperfect

For all have sinned and fall short of the glory of God . . . ROMANS 3:23 (NKJV)

Reflection: No one will walk this earth and be free of sin. We're human. But falling is not failing! God loves you as you are. You can always pick yourself up and keep going.

What have you ever failed at, then looked to God to help you through?

_____

_____

_____

_____

_____

BLESSINGS _____

_____

_____

_____

_____

_____

_____

_____

God Will Bring You Joy

These things I have spoken to you, that My joy may remain in you, and that your joy may be full. JOHN 15:11 (NKJV)

Reflection: Sometimes we can become so angry about a situation that we allow it to remove our joy. Something God has created cannot be taken from you; it is only masked for the fleeting moment. His joy remains with you always.

What's been hindering your joy?

_____

_____

_____

_____

_____

THANKS _____

_____

_____

_____

_____

_____

_____

Building You Up

Through wisdom a house is built, And by understanding it is established; By knowledge the rooms are filled With all precious and pleasant riches. PROVERBS 24:3–4 (NKJV)

Reflection: Think of your life this way: Through salvation you are made whole. Through service you are filled with love, peace, and hope. With wisdom, you receive understanding.

Where do you see salvation, service, and wisdom in your life?

_____

_____

_____

_____

_____

GUIDANCE _____

_____

_____

_____

_____

_____

_____

_____

_____

Overcoming Difficult Times

Humble yourselves, therefore, under the mighty hand of God so that at the proper time he may exalt you, casting all your anxieties on him, because he cares for you. 1 PETER 5:6–7 (ESV)

Reflection: Glory to God! Hallelujah! Shout these praises knowing God will care for and exalt you. God carries your worries and your anxieties in the palm of His hand, so you can overcome them.

Have you felt anxious recently? If so, will you put that to God so that He can take care of you?

_____

_____

_____

_____

_____

PRAYER REQUESTS _____

_____

_____

_____

_____

_____

_____

_____

Blessings Produced by Believing

Blessed is she who believed, for there will be a fulfillment of those things which were told her from the Lord. LUKE 1:45 (NKJV)

Reflection: God will always come through. We can ask God to repair our relationship and He will do it. We can ask God to protect and comfort us and He will do it. God is always listening; He just wants us to believe.

Do you believe God is capable of repairing what is broken in your life?

_____

_____

_____

_____

_____

BLESSINGS ——————————————————————

_____

_____

_____

_____

_____

_____

_____

_____

Making Mistakes

I do not understand what I do. For what I want to do I do not do, but what I hate I do. ROMANS 7:15 (NIV)

Reflection: We all make mistakes and fall short. Take comfort in knowing God is with you no matter what. Just dust yourself off and keep going forward.

Do you sometimes feel uncertainty about knowing right from wrong? What do you do if you make the wrong choice?

_____

_____

_____

_____

_____

THANKS _____

_____

_____

_____

_____

_____

_____

_____

It's All Good

Come now, let us reason together, says the Lord: though your sins are like scarlet, they shall be as white as snow; though they are red like crimson, they shall become like wool. ISAIAH 1:18 (ESV)

Reflection: Knocking over piled blocks, spilling paint on a clean floor. Frustrating—but can a child do anything truly unforgivable? No. God is that forgiving parent, and we are the child. No sin is too great for Him to not forgive.

What experience have you had recently where God revealed His presence? When have you felt He bore your sins for you?

_____

_____

_____

_____

_____

GUIDANCE _____

_____

_____

_____

_____

_____

_____

God Helps You Face Anything

Strength and honor are her clothing; She shall rejoice in time to come.
PROVERBS 31:25 (NKJV)

Reflection: With God by your side, you can laugh in the face of trouble and smile in the midst of danger. God holds you in His arms tightly, and because of that, you are able to face anything.

What can you face today with God by your side?

_____

_____

_____

_____

_____

PRAYER REQUESTS

_____

_____

_____

_____

_____

_____

_____

_____

Just a Phone Call Away

Call upon me in the day of trouble; I will deliver you, and you shall glorify me. PSALM 50:15 (NKJV)

Reflection: God wants you to know that regardless of any temporary disconnections you may be experiencing, He is the ultimate connection.

Who do you call on first when you feel disconnected? Does God lead you to someone to discuss your troubles with? Who?

_____

_____

_____

_____

_____

BLESSINGS _____

_____

_____

_____

_____

_____

_____

_____

Good Work

And let us consider how to stir up one another to love and good works . . .
HEBREWS 10:24 (ESV)

Reflection: There are so many wonderful organizations and churches that provide volunteer opportunities. When you are doing the good work, do not forget to bring friends and family. The good work is better when shared.

Where do you volunteer, and do you share this work with others?

THANKS

Honesty Is Release

He who covers his sins will not prosper, But whoever confesses and forsakes them will have mercy. PROVERBS 28:13 (NKJV)

Reflection: Sometimes embarrassment can cause us to try to cover up our mistakes and sins. The cover up creates another . . . and another. While difficult at times, life is better lived with honesty.

Does sin cause you to feel embarrassed? How can you show more honesty?

_____

_____

_____

_____

_____

GUIDANCE _____

_____

_____

_____

_____

_____

_____

_____

Strength in Times of Adversity

The Lord also will be a refuge for the oppressed, A refuge in times of trouble. PSALM 9:9 (NKJV)

Reflection: With everything going on, it sometimes can feel like the world is upon your shoulders. During times of trouble and pain, try to relax and take refuge in Jesus. He will carry your burdens.

When was a time you took refuge in Jesus? How long did it take for you to turn to Him?

_____

_____

_____

_____

_____

PRAYER REQUESTS _____

_____

_____

_____

_____

_____

_____

_____

You Are Special

We remember before our God and Father your work produced by faith, your labor prompted by love, and your endurance inspired by hope in our Lord Jesus Christ. 1 THESSALONIANS 1:3 (NIV)

Reflection: Take a seed, water it, give it sun, and you'll get a flower. You work and get results. It's tangible. The work you put into growing God's kingdom might not be something you can see and touch, but He knows, and loves, every step.

How has God revealed to you that you are special to Him?

_____

_____

_____

_____

_____

BLESSINGS ———————————————————————————

_____

_____

_____

_____

_____

_____

You Are Chosen

For you are a people holy to the Lord your God. Out of all the peoples on the face of the earth, the Lord has chosen you to be his treasured possession. DEUTERONOMY 14:2 (NIV)

Reflection: You are chosen. Your flaws and imperfections are invisible to God. You, personally, are a treasure. He chooses *you*.

How is your life better with God in it? What can you do to show your appreciation?

_____

_____

_____

_____

_____

THANKS _____

_____

_____

_____

_____

_____

_____

_____

Shine Bright Like a Star

Those who are wise will shine like the brightness of the heavens, and those who lead many to righteousness, like the stars for ever and ever.
DANIEL 12:3 (NIV)

Reflection: God sees you as His precious gem. Let your star shine bright.

When have you shined like a bright star? What did it bring to your life?

_____

_____

_____

_____

_____

GUIDANCE _____

_____

_____

_____

_____

_____

_____

_____

_____

_____

The Greatest Speaker

And he said, "O man greatly loved, fear not, peace be with you; be strong and of good courage." And as he spoke to me, I was strengthened and said, "Let my lord speak, for you have strengthened me." DANIEL 10:19 (ESV)

Reflection: Sometimes you don't even notice a prayer has been answered until you reflect and realize you might have been praying for the wrong thing . . . that God gave you what you needed and not necessarily what you thought you wanted.

When have you been given more than you asked for?

_____

_____

_____

_____

_____

PRAYER REQUESTS ⎯⎯⎯⎯⎯⎯⎯⎯⎯⎯⎯⎯⎯⎯⎯

_____

_____

_____

_____

_____

_____

_____

Coming Short

Surely there is not a righteous man on earth who does good and never sins. ECCLESIASTES 7:20 (ESV)

Reflection: No one is free of sin. We all have sinned and will continue to sin throughout life. This does not make you a bad person, nor does it mean you do not love God. It means you are human.

Do you sometimes doubt God's forgiveness? How has God revealed forgiveness to you?

_____

_____

_____

_____

_____

BLESSINGS _____

_____

_____

_____

_____

_____

_____

Size Does Not Matter

Then David put his hand in his bag and took out a stone; and he slung it and struck the Philistine in his forehead, so that the stone sank into his forehead, and he fell on his face to the earth. 1 SAMUEL 17:49 (NKJV)

Reflection: Small David beat the giant Goliath because his faith was even bigger than his body. God does not look for the strongest or the tallest. He's looking for the most faithful. Could He be looking for you?

How do you use your faith to give you strength? Has it helped beat a Goliath?

_____

_____

_____

_____

_____

THANKS _____

_____

_____

_____

_____

_____

_____

Sorrow No Longer

My soul melts away for sorrow; strengthen me according to your word!
PSALM 119:28 (ESV)

Reflection: Grieving a loss can take a long time. Our Lord might not be able to take away our sorrow completely, but knowing He is walking with us, holding our hand, can be very comforting.

When was a time you felt broken and God helped you feel whole again?

_____

_____

_____

_____

_____

_____

GUIDANCE _____

_____

_____

_____

_____

_____

_____

_____

_____

_____

Walking into Your Future

See then that you walk circumspectly, not as fools but as wise, redeeming the time, because the days are evil. Therefore do not be unwise, but understand what the will of the Lord is. EPHESIANS 5:15–17 (NKJV)

Reflection: Allowing a closed door to stay shut makes room for a new one to be opened. Opening a door that's been closed only revisits the past. Open a new one and walk into your future!

Is there something from your past you feel stuck on? How can you close that door?

_____

_____

_____

_____

_____

PRAYER REQUESTS _____

_____

_____

_____

_____

_____

_____

Forgiving Together

To him all the prophets bear witness that everyone who believes in him receives forgiveness of sins through his name. ACTS 10:43 (ESV)

Reflection: If God is always forgiving all of us, shouldn't we also be always trying to forgive one another, too? God's endless forgiveness can inspire us to extend the same to others.

How do you approach sinful hurt against you?

_____

_____

_____

_____

_____

BLESSINGS _____

_____

_____

_____

_____

_____

_____

_____

_____

Stay Connected

Whoever isolates himself seeks his own desire; he breaks out against all sound judgment. PROVERBS 18:1 (ESV)

Reflection: God does not want you to isolate yourself from others. Isolation can cause a person to be selfish, instead of selfless. It is why we gather with others to praise Him, study Him, and celebrate Him.

Who do you gather with to praise God? What does that community give your life?

_____

_____

_____

_____

_____

THANKS _____

_____

_____

_____

_____

_____

_____

_____

Goodness of God

The Lord is good, a stronghold in the day of trouble; he knows those who take refuge in him. NAHUM 1:7 (ESV)

Reflection: The goodness of God can remove all troubles because He is your stronghold. When you are faced with adversity, do not fret, because God is with you. This verse informs you how God knows when you take refuge in Him.

What do you do when you are faced with trouble?

_____

_____

_____

_____

_____

GUIDANCE _____

_____

_____

_____

_____

_____

_____

_____

_____

God Will Fight for You

The Lord will fight for you, and you shall hold your peace.
EXODUS 14:14 (NKJV)

Reflection: As a little kid you probably often fought with siblings and friends and even parents. You had a lot of emotions inside and it was hard to restrain them. As an adult though, you've learned the importance of keeping calm. Offering your frustration up to God while counting to 10 is one way to keep your cool.

Have you been in a combative situation recently? How did you handle it?

_____

_____

_____

_____

_____

PRAYER REQUESTS _____

_____

_____

_____

_____

_____

Speaking with Kindness

She opens her mouth with wisdom, And on her tongue is the law of kindness. PROVERBS 31:26 (NKJV)

Reflection: Sometimes taking 10 seconds before speaking can change an entire conversation. The subject in Proverbs 31 always ensures her mouth is a tool of goodness, love, peace, and hope, and in return, one that is treasured.

Do you try to think before you speak? What positive things does it help you say? What negative things does it prevent you from saying?

_____

_____

_____

_____

_____

BLESSINGS _____

_____

_____

_____

_____

_____

_____

Be Kind

Be kindly affectionate to one another with brotherly love, in honor giving preference to one another . . . ROMANS 12:10 (NKJV)

Reflection: We can serve and honor one another by being kind and affectionate through hugs and assuring pats on the back or shoulder. We can also uplift each other through encouraging words.

Have you shown kindness to someone recently? Has someone shown you kindness recently? How did it feel? Did you feel closer to God?

_____

_____

_____

_____

_____

THANKS ⎯⎯⎯⎯⎯⎯⎯⎯⎯⎯⎯⎯⎯⎯⎯⎯⎯⎯⎯

_____

_____

_____

_____

_____

_____

_____

Wings to Soar

But they who wait for the Lord shall renew their strength; they shall mount up with wings like eagles; they shall run and not be weary; they shall walk and not faint. ISAIAH 40:31 (ESV)

Reflection: During your season of weariness, be patient. God will have you soar past your expectations.

How can you build a foundation strong enough to be able to soar?

_____

_____

_____

_____

_____

GUIDANCE _____

_____

_____

_____

_____

_____

_____

_____

_____

_____

Listening to Understand

Whoever restrains his words has knowledge, and he who has a cool spirit is a man of understanding. PROVERBS 17:27 (ESV)

Reflection: Strength is not always in what you express, but what you do not express.

Have you ever had the opportunity to say something, but didn't, and were glad you didn't? What would have happened if you did?

_____

_____

_____

_____

_____

_____

PRAYER REQUESTS _____

_____

_____

_____

_____

_____

_____

_____

_____

Leaping over Obstacles

The Lord God is my strength; He will make my feet like deer's feet, And He will make me walk on my high hills. HABAKKUK 3:19 (NKJV)

Reflection: God will allow you to leap over obstacles like a deer leaps over tall grass. The only way to get a beautiful view from the mountaintop is by making the climb. The obstacles in your path have made you stronger!

With God's help, what obstacles are you leaping over? How does He give you strength to move past your troubles?

_____

_____

_____

_____

_____

BLESSINGS

_____

_____

_____

_____

_____

_____

Always Focused

Have you not known? Have you not heard? The everlasting God, the Lord, The Creator of the ends of the earth, Neither faints nor is weary. His understanding is unsearchable. ISAIAH 40:28 (NKJV)

Reflection: God is always focused on us, His children. He never turns His back on you.

What deters you from being focused on God? What can you do to focus on Him more?

_____

_____

_____

_____

_____

THANKS ————————————————————————

_____

_____

_____

_____

_____

_____

_____

Temptation Will Not Overtake You

No temptation has overtaken you except what is common to mankind. And God is faithful; he will not let you be tempted beyond what you can bear. But when you are tempted, he will also provide a way out so that you can endure it. 1 CORINTHIANS 10:13 (NIV)

Reflection: Life is full of temptations. No one is perfect, but through faith and by looking to God, we can overcome these temptations.

What are you being tempted with in life? How has God helped you avoid the temptation?

_____

_____

_____

_____

_____

GUIDANCE _____

_____

_____

_____

_____

_____

_____

Prayer Soothes

But let him ask in faith, with no doubting, for the one who doubts is like a wave of the sea that is driven and tossed by the wind. JAMES 1:6 (ESV)

Reflection: Dear God, as I faithfully pray before you, grant me patience. In today's fast-paced world, it is hard to wait. I ask you to not see my impatience as doubt. Help me to stand firm in knowing there is nothing you can't do. Amen.

When was the last time you got impatient about a prayer request?

_____

_____

_____

_____

_____

PRAYER REQUESTS _____

_____

_____

_____

_____

_____

_____

_____

No Longer Afraid

When I am afraid, I put my trust in you. PSALM 56:3 (NIV)

Reflection: When I feel fear, help me put my trust in Jesus. I know He will remove the fear that's troubling me. Jesus, I trust you. Amen.

What are you fearful of in your life? How will you deal with the fear?

_____

_____

_____

_____

_____

BLESSINGS ━━━━━━━━━━━━━━━━━━━━━━━━━━━━━━━

_____

_____

_____

_____

_____

_____

_____

_____

_____

Got Your Back

Iron sharpens iron, and one man sharpens another. PROVERBS 27:17 (ESV)

Reflection: Two people together walking in Christ are able to do more than just one. By building relationships with others of God, we can grow together in His name.

Who are you sharpening? Who sharpens you?

_____

_____

_____

_____

_____

THANKS _____

_____

_____

_____

_____

_____

_____

_____

_____

You Are Mighty

Finally, be strong in the Lord and in the strength of his might.
EPHESIANS 6:10 (ESV)

Reflection: God makes you mighty daily. He wakes you up every day because He believes in you. You are mighty because mighty is He who lives in you.

Who in your life reminds you to never give up? Think of ways you can quietly thank them, either through prayer, words, or service.

GUIDANCE

Cherish the Day

So teach us to number our days that we may get a heart of wisdom.
PSALM 90:12 (ESV)

Reflection: We all know the saying, "live every day as if it is your last." As we grow up and go through life, we realize how true this is. Each day has meaning. Do you think the more you serve the Lord the better those days will be?

How will you cherish today and serve the Lord?

_____

_____

_____

_____

_____

PRAYER REQUESTS _____

_____

_____

_____

_____

_____

_____

_____

_____

Determined with Love

May the Lord direct your hearts into God's love and Christ's perseverance.
2 THESSALONIANS 3:5 (NIV)

Reflection: God is determined to direct your hearts toward His everlasting love. Love is dedicating your life to God and being able to express your love to Him.

How can you use God's love to persevere the next time you experience something difficult?

BLESSINGS

Do Good

Trust in the Lord, and do good; dwell in the land and befriend faithfulness.
PSALM 37:3 (ESV)

Reflection: "Doing good" is an important aspect of being a Christian. You can show the Lord you trust Him by doing good unto others. It could be in the form of being kind to strangers, helping a friend, or volunteering in our community.

Think of a recent time you did something good. How did it feel? Did you feel closer to the Lord?

_____

_____

_____

_____

_____

THANKS ⎯⎯⎯⎯⎯⎯⎯⎯⎯⎯⎯⎯⎯⎯⎯⎯⎯⎯⎯

_____

_____

_____

_____

_____

_____

Rest After the Work

Come to Me, all you who labor and are heavy laden, and I will give you rest.
MATTHEW 11:28 (NKJV)

Reflection: Hectic days, busy schedules. We all have them. Go to God when you are feeling tired and rest with Him. Making time for restful habits like journaling, meditating, or praying can bring some peace and calm to your busy days.

Have you been feeling tired or down lately? Did you look to God for rest? How did you feel after giving yourself a break?

_____

_____

_____

_____

_____

GUIDANCE _____

_____

_____

_____

_____

_____

_____

_____

Fight the Good Fight

Fight the good fight of the faith. Take hold of the eternal life to which you were called and about which you made the good confession in the presence of many witnesses. 1 TIMOTHY 6:12 (ESV)

Reflection: Dear Lord, help me fight the good fight. My life is a story of faith. Though I may stumble on the way, help me to keep fighting, and to stand strong in my faith. In Jesus's name, Amen.

What does fighting the good fight mean to you? Have you had to defend your faith before? How did you stand strong?

_____

_____

_____

_____

_____

PRAYER REQUESTS ————————————————————————

_____

_____

_____

_____

_____

_____

_____

_____

No False Claims

Whoever claims to love God yet hates a brother or sister is a liar. For whoever does not love their brother and sister, whom they have seen, cannot love God, whom they have not seen. 1 JOHN 4:20 (NIV)

Reflection: We cannot claim our love for God but have hate for other people. We are all made in His image; disliking others is the same as disliking Him.

Is there hate you may feel toward someone that you can work to change to love? How can God help?

_____

_____

_____

_____

_____

BLESSINGS ———————————————————————————————

_____

_____

_____

_____

_____

_____

_____

Not Discouraged but Encouraged

Have I not commanded you? Be strong and courageous. Do not be frightened, and do not be dismayed, for the Lord your God is with you wherever you go. JOSHUA 1:9 (ESV)

Reflection: God is your biggest cheerleader; cheering you on through ups and downs. Whether a roof or relationship needs to be repaired, an agenda or stack of laundry needs to be tackled, God is there to root for you.

Where do you need God most in your life right now?

_____

_____

_____

_____

_____

THANKS ─────────────────────────

_____

_____

_____

_____

_____

_____

Power of the Tongue

There is one who speaks like the piercings of a sword, But the tongue of the wise promotes health. PROVERBS 12:18 (NKJV)

Reflection: Remember the phrase, "sticks and stones may break my bones, but words can never hurt me"? News flash! Words hurt. They can cut deep. The good news is that kind words have a great impact, too.

What are some kind words you can tell someone today? Who needs them?

_____

_____

_____

_____

_____

GUIDANCE _____

_____

_____

_____

_____

_____

_____

_____

_____

Focus on Faith

Seek the Lord and his strength; seek his presence continually!
1 CHRONICLES 16:11 (ESV)

Reflection: Our fast-paced, modern lives can often distract us from our faith. Sometimes we need to put down our phone, turn off the TV, and unplug the computer. Staying focused can be hard but making time for our faith is a great way to nurture it.

Have you felt distracted lately? How can you better nurture your faith right now?

_____

_____

_____

_____

_____

PRAYER REQUESTS _____

_____

_____

_____

_____

_____

_____

Build Your Foundation

Cast your cares on the Lord and he will sustain you; he will never let the righteous be shaken. PSALM 55:22 (NIV)

Reflection: Everyone has bad days. Maybe even a couple in a row! The beauty of faith is knowing you're not alone.

Make a list of woes to hand over to God today so you can focus on the good stuff.

_____

_____

_____

_____

_____

BLESSINGS _____

_____

_____

_____

_____

_____

_____

_____

_____

One Day at a Time

Therefore do not be anxious about tomorrow, for tomorrow will be anxious for itself. Sufficient for the day is its own trouble. MATTHEW 6:34 (ESV)

Reflection: Congratulations, you've made it through another day! Don't sweat what's going to happen tomorrow. Try to slow down and focus on the now by taking it one day at a time.

Are you worrying about tomorrow? How can God help you be present today?

_____

_____

_____

_____

_____

THANKS _____

_____

_____

_____

_____

_____

_____

_____

_____

Through the Valley

Yea, though I walk through the valley of the shadow of death, I will fear no evil; For You are with me; Your rod and Your staff, they comfort me.
PSALM 23:4 (NKJV)

Reflection: It's okay to feel scared. Bills, aging parents, angry bosses . . . it can get to us. The way through it is knowing God is walking with us, holding our hand, never leaving our side.

What valley has God helped you make it through?

_____

_____

_____

_____

_____

GUIDANCE _____

_____

_____

_____

_____

_____

_____

_____

Plans in Sight

However, as it is written: "What no eye has seen, what no ear has heard, and what no human mind has conceived"—the things God has prepared for those who love him... 1 CORINTHIANS 2:9 (NIV)

Reflection: Have you ever done a 500-piece puzzle? Cooked a three-course meal? In the middle of it, it may have been hard to see the end—but you knew it was there. Just like trusting that end was there, we can trust God's plans for us are in motion.

What was something you did recently that you are proud of? Did you struggle to see the end? Did God help?

_____

_____

_____

_____

_____

PRAYER REQUESTS ━━━━━━━━━━━━━━━━━━━━━━━━━━━

_____

_____

_____

_____

_____

_____

_____

Woes Won't Last

Let not your hearts be troubled. Believe in God; believe also in me.
JOHN 14:1 (ESV)

Reflection: You know when someone says a struggle might have come into your life for a reason? Maybe it has, maybe not. But that perspective takes the focus off the pain and places it toward growth. Even if it wasn't planned, the growth can bring you closer to God.

What troubles has God brought you out of? How can God assist you in your present troubles? Write down your troubles and tell God what you need Him to do.

_____

_____

_____

_____

_____

BLESSINGS ————————————————————————

_____

_____

_____

_____

_____

_____

_____

Remaining Selfless

Let nothing be done through selfish ambition or conceit, but in lowliness of mind let each esteem others better than himself. Let each of you look out not only for his own interests, but also for the interests of others.
PHILIPPIANS 2:3–4 (NKJV)

Reflection: Blessed are those who help others with no intention of personal gain.

Have you experienced a selfless act recently? How did it feel to be on the receiving end? How can you put that back out into the world?

_____

_____

_____

_____

_____

THANKS _____

_____

_____

_____

_____

_____

_____

_____

_____

You Against the World

I have said these things to you, that in me you may have peace. In the world you will have tribulation. But take heart; I have overcome the world. JOHN 16:33 (ESV)

Reflection: Life can be hard and unfair. God will give you strength to face life's difficulties and help find the answers you are seeking.

What are you trying to overcome in your walk with Christ? How do you embrace the hand you've been dealt?

_____

_____

_____

_____

_____

GUIDANCE

_____

_____

_____

_____

_____

_____

_____

_____

We Are All Children of God

See what great love the Father has lavished on us, that we should be called children of God! And that is what we are! 1 JOHN 3:1 (NIV)

Reflection: God loves us so much that He calls us His children. We are part of His family. Smile knowing you are loved.

Have you ever been called a child of God? If so, how did you feel? Do you see others as children of God?

_____

_____

_____

_____

_____

PRAYER REQUESTS _____

_____

_____

_____

_____

_____

_____

_____

_____

_____

The Savior

When Peter came to himself, he said, "Now I am sure that the Lord has sent his angel and rescued me from the hand of Herod and from all that the Jewish people were expecting." ACTS 12:11 (ESV)

Reflection: Some people need a miracle to be reminded or convinced there is a God, but is that really faith? It is comforting to be able to walk with Him daily.

Write about the time when you accepted God into your heart.

_____

_____

_____

_____

_____

BLESSINGS ————————————————————————

_____

_____

_____

_____

_____

_____

_____

_____

Blessings from God

Blessed is the man who trusts in the Lord, whose trust is the Lord.
He is like a tree planted by water, that sends out its roots by the stream,
and does not fear when heat comes, for its leaves remain green, and is
not anxious in the year of drought, for it does not cease to bear fruit.
JEREMIAH 17:7–8 (ESV)

Reflection: Seasons of drought come and go, but God is still in the blessing business! The rain will come. It might be a few sprinkles here and there but trust that you will be refreshed.

Do you feel you are in a drought? Where can you look to see God's blessings?

_____

_____

_____

_____

_____

THANKS ━━━━━━━━━━━━━━━━━━━━━

_____

_____

_____

_____

_____

Love Not Fear

There is no fear in love, but perfect love casts out fear. For fear has to do with punishment, and whoever fears has not been perfected in love.
1 JOHN 4:18 (ESV)

Reflection: God has never meant for love to hurt nor cause you fear. Relationships based on fear are not true, loving relationships. Never allow love to keep you from peace.

Does fear sometimes hinder your love from flourishing? What have you done to cast it out?

_____

_____

_____

_____

_____

GUIDANCE _____

_____

_____

_____

_____

_____

_____

No Doubt

My flesh and my heart fail; But God is the strength of my heart and my portion forever. PSALM 73:26 (NKJV)

Reflection: With age comes dealing with ailments of our mind and body, but not our soul. Our faith is one thing that will get better with age!

How can you work to strengthen your soul? Do you feel your faith getting better with age?

PRAYER REQUESTS

God Will Strengthen You

But the Lord stood with me and strengthened me, so that the message might be preached fully through me . . . 2 TIMOTHY 4:17 (NKJV)

Reflection: Sharing God's word doesn't have to mean using a megaphone to shout from street corners. It can simply mean leading by example. Use the strength within you to spread the Gospel.

How do you spread the Gospel?

_____

_____

_____

_____

_____

BLESSINGS _____

_____

_____

_____

_____

_____

_____

_____

_____

The Possibilities Are Endless

For with God nothing will be impossible. LUKE 1:37 (NKJV)

Reflection: When the world gives you a no, God will give you a yes.

When did the world give you a no, but God gave you a yes?

_____

_____

_____

_____

_____

THANKS _____

_____

_____

_____

_____

_____

_____

_____

_____

_____

Practicing Prayer

Whoever trusts in his own mind is a fool, but he who walks in wisdom will be delivered. PROVERBS 28:26 (ESV)

Reflection: Life doesn't come with instructions. We get plenty of lessons, we learn by observing others, and the rest we figure out along the way. We get better as we go, and with practice. Prayer is like that, too. There is no right or wrong way to do it, but practice makes us better, wiser, and more fulfilled.

Do you practice your prayer? What do you think you benefit from regularly praying?

_____

_____

_____

_____

_____

GUIDANCE _____

_____

_____

_____

_____

_____

_____

You Are the Clay

But now, O Lord, You are our Father; We are the clay, and You our potter; And all we are the work of Your hand. ISAIAH 64:8 (NKJV)

Reflection: God is the potter who shaped you in His image. He is still shaping your soul. When life gets hectic, when you make mistakes, when you feel you don't deserve forgiveness, remember you aren't finished yet.

How has God shaped your life?

_____

_____

_____

_____

_____

PRAYER REQUESTS _____

_____

_____

_____

_____

_____

_____

_____

Loving Him

And we know that in all things God works for the good of those who love him, who have been called according to his purpose. ROMANS 8:28 (NIV)

Reflection: We want what's best for our friends and family, because we love them. If they ask us for help, we happily give it to them. Imagine how much greater God's love is for us, and how happy He wants us to be!

When did you realize how much God loved you? Were you able to return the love to Him?

_____

_____

_____

_____

_____

BLESSINGS _____

_____

_____

_____

_____

_____

_____

Love Hard

And you shall love the Lord your God with all your heart and with all your soul and with all your mind and with all your strength. MARK 12:30 (ESV)

Reflection: God loves us unconditionally, through good and bad. We can use Him as our example for how to love Him back.

How do you show your love for God?

_____

_____

_____

_____

_____

_____

THANKS ━━━━━━━━━━━━━━━━━━━━━━━━━━━

_____

_____

_____

_____

_____

_____

_____

_____

_____

_____

Prayer Can Remove Doubt

And have mercy on those who doubt . . . JUDE 1:22 (ESV)

Reflection: Your doubt can deter you from moving forward toward your destiny. The key to removing doubt is through prayer. Pray to the Lord for guidance and answers to carry you through the toughest days.

What prayers are you saying today for guidance and answers?

_____

_____

_____

_____

_____

GUIDANCE _____

_____

_____

_____

_____

_____

_____

_____

_____

Be Not Superficial

Your beauty should not come from outward adornment, such as elabo-rate hairstyles and the wearing of gold jewelry or fine clothes. Rather, it should be that of your inner self, the unfading beauty of a gentle and quiet spirit, which is of great worth in God's sight. 1 PETER 3:3–4 (NIV)

Reflection: When we buy material things, they usually only bring temporary satisfaction, perhaps some longer than others. What if we invested an equal amount of time in our spiritual growth?

What can you do today to grow spiritually?

_____

_____

_____

_____

_____

PRAYER REQUESTS _____

_____

_____

_____

_____

_____

_____

_____

_____

Faithful with Little

One who is faithful in a very little is also faithful in much, and one who is dishonest in a very little is also dishonest in much. LUKE 16:10 (ESV)

Reflection: There is no such thing as a little lie; a lie is a lie. However, a little faith *does* exist. God does not require us to have a huge amount of faith. Start with a little and see where that takes you.

What little ways you can strengthen or show God your faith?

_____

_____

_____

_____

_____

_____

BLESSINGS _____

_____

_____

_____

_____

_____

_____

_____

_____

_____

Why Troubled?

He said to them, "Why are you troubled, and why do doubts rise in your minds?" LUKE 24:38 (NIV)

Reflection: The verse asks the question, "Why are you troubled?" There is no reason to accept the troubling feelings of defeat nor doubt. Your coach has never lost a season! He is undefeated—which means you are, too.

What can you do when you feel troubled?

_____

_____

_____

_____

_____

THANKS _____

_____

_____

_____

_____

_____

_____

_____

_____

Difficulties with Faith

Consider it pure joy, my brothers and sisters, whenever you face trials of many kinds, because you know that the testing of your faith produces perseverance. JAMES 1:2–3 (NIV)

Reflection: Loss of friends or family members. Breakups. Financial woes. We have all experienced them . . . and we will again. The test of your faith is not the end of your battle; it is only the beginning.

What did you do the last time your faith was tested?

_____

_____

_____

_____

_____

GUIDANCE _____

_____

_____

_____

_____

_____

_____

_____

_____

_____

Obedience

Children, obey your parents in the Lord, for this is right. "Honor your father and mother," which is the first commandment with promise: "that it may be well with you and you may live long on the earth."
EPHESIANS 6:1–3 (NKJV)

Reflection: God has high expectations of us, but if we fall short, we can always talk to Him and repent. To enter His kingdom, communication is the key; forgiveness is the door.

As a child, did you disobey your parents? How many times did they forgive you?

PRAYER REQUESTS _____

A Filling Better Than Pie

Now may the God of hope fill you with all joy and peace in believing,
that you may abound in hope by the power of the Holy Spirit.
ROMANS 15:13 (NKJV)

Reflection: A pie can be filled with all kinds of things. Depending on the crust, you might not know what's inside. With God we always know the type of filling, or feeling. God fills us up with joy, peace, love, and so much more.

What are some of the more hidden or unseen ways God has filled your life?

_____

_____

_____

_____

_____

BLESSINGS ━━━━━━━━━━━━━━━━━━━━━━━━━━━━━━━━

_____

_____

_____

_____

_____

_____

_____

Because You Know He's Real

Jesus said to him, "Have you believed because you have seen me? Blessed are those who have not seen and yet have believed."
JOHN 20:29 (ESV)

Reflection: God can be felt, heard, and seen everywhere—the pink of the sky, the feel of a breeze near the ocean, the whistling of the birds.

What can you do today to see signs of Jesus's existence?

_____

_____

_____

_____

_____

_____

THANKS ————————————————————————————

_____

_____

_____

_____

_____

_____

_____

_____

_____

Choosing Peace

For God has not given us a spirit of fear, but of power and of love and of a sound mind. 2 TIMOTHY 1:7 (NKJV)

Reflection: It's not always easy, but we can choose peace in the midst of chaos. It might take concentrated prayer and faith, but the choice is ours.

Why does fear try to invade love?

_____

_____

_____

_____

_____

GUIDANCE _____

_____

_____

_____

_____

_____

_____

_____

_____

_____

_____

Eyes Opened

Oh, taste and see that the Lord is good; Blessed is the man who trusts in Him! PSALM 34:8 (NKJV)

Reflection: Lord, open my eye, to taste the goodness of the Lord. God poured blessings upon me at my worst and at my best. Though I may have not seen His blessings at the time, I see them now. God is good!

What are some of the greatest gifts God has given you?

_____

_____

_____

_____

_____

PRAYER REQUESTS ⸻⸻⸻⸻⸻⸻⸻

_____

_____

_____

_____

_____

_____

_____

_____

Your Spirit Is Everlasting

For he who sows to his flesh will of the flesh reap corruption, but he who sows to the Spirit will of the Spirit reap everlasting life. GALATIANS 6:8 (NKJV)

Reflection: Today's focus on material goods, social media, and celebrity can feel overwhelming. Why follow these things when you can follow God?

Think of some ways you can spend less time in the material world and more time with your faith.

_____

_____

_____

_____

_____

BLESSINGS ━━━━━━━━━━━━━━━━━━━━━━━━━━━━━━━━━

_____

_____

_____

_____

_____

_____

_____

_____

The Kingdom Is Waiting

But seek first the kingdom of God and His righteousness, and all these things shall be added to you. MATTHEW 6:33 (NKJV)

Reflection: The kingdom is ready for you. Are you getting ready for it?

What gifts has God blessed you with to use in the kingdom of God?

_____

_____

_____

_____

_____

_____

THANKS _____

_____

_____

_____

_____

_____

_____

_____

_____

Do Not Become Consumed

Because of the Lord's great love we are not consumed, for his compassions never fail. LAMENTATIONS 3:22 (NIV)

Reflection: Missed payments, forgotten appointments, fights with friends . . . we've all experienced challenges with different things in life. God's great love will not allow you to become consumed with the wiles of the world.

What do you do when doubt sets in your mind?

_____

_____

_____

_____

_____

GUIDANCE _____

_____

_____

_____

_____

_____

_____

_____

_____

He Is King

Be still, and know that I am God; I will be exalted among the nations, I will be exalted in the earth! PSALM 46:10 (ESV)

Reflection: God wants us to be still, so we can hear Him. God is looking forward to being your success story. Let Him do His job.

What do you need to do to be still and allow God to speak to you? What job do you think He is trying to do?

_____

_____

_____

_____

_____

_____

PRAYER REQUESTS _____

_____

_____

_____

_____

_____

_____

_____

Choose Words Carefully

Set a watch, O Lord, before my mouth; keep the door of my lips.
PSALM 141:3 (KJV)

Reflection: We've all said things we wish we didn't. Words can't be unspoken, but apologies are always welcomed. It's never too late to reach out and patch things up.

Who can you apologize to for regretted words spoken in anger? Ask the Holy Spirit for guidance on what to say.

_____

_____

_____

_____

_____

BLESSINGS _____

_____

_____

_____

_____

_____

_____

_____

Hope, Patience, and Faithfulness Lead the Way

Be joyful in hope, patient in affliction, faithful in prayer. ROMANS 12:12 (NIV)

Reflection: The triple threat to conquer a stressful day: hope for the best, patience through the mess, and faithfulness will pass the test.

How do you use hope, patience, and faithfulness to get through a rough day?

_____

_____

_____

_____

_____

_____

THANKS —————————————————————————

_____

_____

_____

_____

_____

_____

_____

_____

His Presence

Fear not, for I am with you; be not dismayed, for I am your God; I will strengthen you, I will help you, I will uphold you with my righteous right hand. ISAIAH 41:10 (ESV)

Reflection: When you were a child, your parents held your hand to keep you safe. God does the same thing—He holds your hand to show you love and keep you safe. He's holding it right now!

What will you do to keep God near you?

_____

_____

_____

_____

_____

GUIDANCE ———————————————————

_____

_____

_____

_____

_____

_____

_____

_____

_____

Ignoring Fools

The words of a wise man's mouth are gracious, But the lips of a fool shall swallow him up . . . ECCLESIASTES 10:12 (NKJV)

Reflection: Jesus always has our best interest at heart, but the people around us might not. If we listen to our faith, we can ignore bad advice or negative words.

How do you positively deal with those who use negative words toward you? Do you have a favorite saying you repeat to yourself when you're feeling down?

_____

_____

_____

_____

_____

PRAYER REQUESTS ━━━━━━━━━━━━━━━━━━━━━━━━━━━━

_____

_____

_____

_____

_____

_____

_____

_____

The Company You Keep

Do not be deceived: "Bad company ruins good morals."
1 CORINTHIANS 15:33 (ESV)

Reflection: The company you keep can either uplift you or bring you down. Surrounding yourself with good, godly people makes it easier to make good choices.

Whose company can you give less attention to because they bring you down? Whose company can you give more attention to because it lifts you up?

_____

_____

_____

_____

_____

BLESSINGS _____

_____

_____

_____

_____

_____

_____

_____

A Wait Never Tasted Better

I say to myself, "The Lord is my portion; therefore I will wait for him."
LAMENTATIONS 3:24 (NIV)

Reflection: Picture it: You're going to your favorite restaurant. You arrive and there is a long wait for a table, but you wait it out. It turns out to be the best meal you've ever had. God's grace is just like that—worth the wait!

Write about a time when you waited a long time for something that paid off in the end.

_____

_____

_____

_____

_____

THANKS ————————————————————————

_____

_____

_____

_____

_____

_____

_____

At the Lord's Pace

Wait for the Lord; be strong, and let your heart take courage; wait for the Lord! PSALM 27:14 (NKJV)

Reflection: The fast pace of the world causes us to be impatient. Racing off to meetings, classes, and appointments. We are always on the go, but allowing the Lord's pace will feel much more relaxing.

Do you feel you're moving a mile a minute right now? How can the Lord help you slow down?

_____

_____

_____

_____

_____

GUIDANCE _____

_____

_____

_____

_____

_____

_____

_____

_____

Keeping Hope

God is in the midst of her, she shall not be moved; God shall help her, just at the break of dawn. PSALM 46:5 (NKJV)

Reflection: Life can be like a workday that feels long, boring, and hard to get through, but we always do. Keep hope that you will make it through.

What is holding your hope hostage? How will you conquer it?

_____

_____

_____

_____

_____

PRAYER REQUESTS ━━━━━━━━━━━━━━━━━━━━

_____

_____

_____

_____

_____

_____

_____

_____

Rejoice in the Lord

The Lord is my strength and my shield; My heart trusted in Him, and I am helped; Therefore my heart greatly rejoices, And with my song I will praise Him. PSALM 28:7 (NKJV)

Reflection: Singing praises can mean sharing your experiences with a friend, especially one who might not be a close follower of Christ. The Lord is your shield to sing His praises!

Do you sing praises for the Lord? Did anyone hear who was not a follower?

BLESSINGS

Teaching the Non-believers

And He marveled because of their unbelief. Then He went about the villages in a circuit, teaching. MARK 6:6 (NKJV)

Reflection: Jesus was not discouraged by those who did not believe Him. Neither should we be discouraged. Outreach is a fulfilling and important part of faith.

Do you participate in outreach in your community? What do you do?

_____

_____

_____

_____

_____

THANKS ——————————————————————————

_____

_____

_____

_____

_____

_____

_____

_____

Call Out His Name

On the day I called, you answered me; my strength of soul you increased.
PSALM 138:3 (ESV)

Reflection: To call on the Lord is a sure thing because His phone is always connected. You can call Him anytime, and He'll listen all day and all night. Don't be afraid to dial.

When have you recently called out to the Lord? What did He say?

_____

_____

_____

_____

_____

GUIDANCE ═══════════════════════════════════════

_____

_____

_____

_____

_____

_____

_____

_____

_____

Follow the Light

Then Jesus spoke to them again, saying, "I am the light of the world.
He who follows Me shall not walk in darkness, but have the light of life."
JOHN 8:12 (NKJV)

Reflection: Jesus is a permanent light, given to us by the best Father ever. If you let His light shine bright enough, you will always know where to turn in your times of darkness.

Have you ever been in a dark place? How did you get out?

_____

_____

_____

_____

_____

PRAYER REQUESTS ▬▬▬▬▬▬▬▬▬▬▬▬▬▬▬

_____

_____

_____

_____

_____

_____

_____

Planting Your Seeds

She considers a field and buys it; From her profits she plants a vineyard. She girds herself with strength, And strengthens her arms.
PROVERBS 31:16–17 (NKJV)

Reflection: Imagine a garden as your future. You can do anything you want with it—will you water and carefully tend to it? The same is true for your faith. You are the only one who can properly tend to your garden.

What seeds have you planted? What are you trying to grow?

_____

_____

_____

_____

_____

BLESSINGS _____

_____

_____

_____

_____

_____

_____

How Great Is God

O God, You are more awesome than Your holy places. The God of Israel is He who gives strength and power to His people. Blessed be God!
PSALM 68:35 (NKJV)

Reflection: Isn't it amazing what you can accomplish with God on your side?

What is an example of God's strength living in you now? Name three of your past accomplishments made possible by God giving you strength.

_____

_____

_____

_____

_____

THANKS _____

_____

_____

_____

_____

_____

_____

_____

Mealtime Joy

Nehemiah said, "Go and enjoy choice food and sweet drinks, and send some to those who have nothing prepared. This day is holy to our Lord. Do not grieve, for the joy of the Lord is your strength." NEHEMIAH 8:10 (NIV)

Reflection: There is nothing quite like sharing a meal with friends and family. It feels good to commune over food and drinks. It can feel even better to share food and drinks with others less fortunate.

Who can you share a meal with today? What do you want to make?

_____

_____

_____

_____

_____

GUIDANCE ━━━━━━━━━━━━━━━━━━━━━━━━━━━━━━

_____

_____

_____

_____

_____

_____

_____

_____

_____

God's Perfect Work

Consider the work of God: who can make straight what he has made crooked? ECCLESIASTES 7:13 (ESV)

Reflection: Today, let the brightness of the sun kiss your face. See how the beauty of the flowers brighten up a space. Watch the natural interaction of two birds singing. This is God's perfect work and it is great.

What creations can you look and listen for today? Tomorrow?

_____

_____

_____

_____

_____

BLESSINGS _____

_____

_____

_____

_____

_____

_____

_____

_____

It Feels Good to Help Others

She extends her hand to the poor, Yes, she reaches out her hands to the needy. She is not afraid of snow for her household, For all her household is clothed with scarlet. PROVERBS 31:20–21 (NKJV)

Reflection: Giving to the needy doesn't always have to be in dollars. Some people donate skills, talents, or simply their time. Get creative! We all have something to give.

What was the most meaningful volunteer work you've experienced? Why?

_____

_____

_____

_____

PRAYER REQUESTS _____

_____

_____

_____

_____

_____

_____

_____

_____

Answered Prayers

Answered Prayers

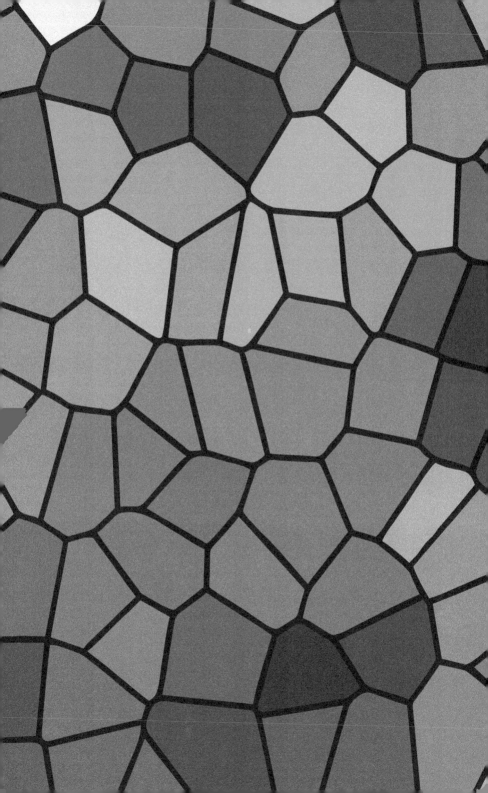

Acknowledgments

I want to acknowledge the women who have always attended my organization, "Beloved Sistah Circle." The world has changed but you all are on my mind and in my heart. I will continue to encourage you all. I share this book with you. I want to acknowledge our amazing "Beloved Sistah" Ms. Dorothy. She left this earth but not my heart. She is one of the most supportive and encouraging women I have met. She is loved and dearly missed. To all my close friends, thank you for your continued support. I want to acknowledge my sister, Jessica Gates, who always supports me in my endeavors. She creates my flyers, pictures, videos, and edits my social media. She is a gem. Jessica, thank you. Last but not least are my young kings of God, Connor and Dylan. They are the best gifts I have ever received. Connor and Dylan are young men of God and keep me focused while holding me accountable.

COPYRIGHT NOTICES

Scripture quotations marked ESV are from The ESV® Bible (The Holy Bible, English Standard Version®). Copyright © 2001 by Crossway, a publishing ministry of Good News Publishers. Used by permission. All rights reserved.

Scripture quotations marked NIV are from the Holy Bible, New International Version®, NIV®. Copyright © 1973, 1978, 1984, 2011 by Biblica, Inc.™ Used by permission of Zondervan. All rights reserved worldwide. Zondervan.com The "NIV" and "New International Version" are trademarks registered in the United States Patent and Trademark Office by Biblica, Inc. ™

Scripture quotations marked NKJV are from the New King James Version®. Copyright © 1982 by Thomas Nelson. Used by permission. All rights reserved.

About the Author

Jocasta Odom is an ordained minister who strives to reach people through motivation, poetry, preaching, and teaching. She is a television host on *Atlanta Live*, formerly starred on *Big Brother*, and her show *That's What's Up* formerly aired on 108 Praise Radio. A certified spiritual life coach, teacher, and author, the most rewarding hat she wears is being the mother of two handsome boys.

CPSIA information can be obtained
at www.ICGtesting.com
Printed in the USA
LVHW011311171220
674419LV00001B/1